Google AdWords for Beginners

Corey Rabazinski

Table of Contents

Introduction

Hello and welcome to Google AdWords for Beginners.

This book was conceived from a need that I noticed while working at a top 100 rated advertising agency, where I ran digital marketing and PPC campaigns for a range of businesses from startups all the way up to Fortune 500 companies.

In order to run a successful campaign it was essential that I had a detailed understanding of the business. This meant I worked closely with organizations and quickly developed an understanding of their internal set up. After just a few months in my position one question kept cropping up. You see, these companies were well organized, highly professional outfits and I kept finding myself asking, 'Why aren't you running these campaigns internally?"

Almost every time I asked, they answered with either 'AdWords is too complicated' or 'we just don't have the time'.

Both answers did not compute for me - especially coming from small businesses. Sure, AdWords has a learning curve, just like most other things and, sure, there is some time needed to manage the campaigns early on, but after seeing it from the other side I couldn't imagine letting another company run my AdWords campaigns.

These businesses had intimate knowledge about their customers and product(s) that could take months or even years for an agency to learn what someone entrenched in the business knew. Whereas learning AdWords should take no more than a weekend and after launching a campaign, management time can be cut to an hour or less a week.

Plus... advertising agencies cost money - sometimes lots of money. Even if the campaigns are delivering results, the management fees can hamstring early stage companies that need the capital.

So knowing this, I decided to write this book to share the fundamentals of running successful AdWords campaigns that I've learned over the years. It is designed for you, a business person, to gather all the knowledge you need to setup and run your own campaign. Some marketers would like you to believe that AdWords is some kind of black magic and they have a special insight that you just don't have. This is not the case. The basics of AdWords is simple, and like I said, you should be able to grasp it in a weekend.

The book is split into eight key areas, which form the framework in which you will build your AdWords campaign. I've kept it simple. No fluff. Just real campaign strategies that have worked for me and can work for you.

The techniques in this book are the same techniques I was using to build successful AdWords campaigns for some of the largest businesses in the world.

I've also created a companion course for this book that has video screencasts from a live AdWords account to show you step-by-step how to implement what you are learning in this book. You can even follow along in your own AdWords account to really retain what you just learned.

The video course is available at www.googleadwordstutorial.com and if you use the coupon code 'BOOK' during the checkout process, you will get 25% off the regular price.

Ok, so enough of that. Let's get into it and start learning AdWords!

Why AdWords?

Ad•words

noun

1. A proven way to reach a large amount of new customers, in any industry, with any budget.

2. A cash-printing machine headquartered in Mountain View, CA.

OK, so I took a few liberties with that definition, but it isn't too far off from reality. Since its launch in 2000, Google's AdWords advertising platform has been a runaway success -both for Google and for the advertisers it enables. The revenue from AdWords is Google's number one source of revenue and continues to grow. In 2013, Google made over $50 billion from advertising alone - far surpassing any other sources.

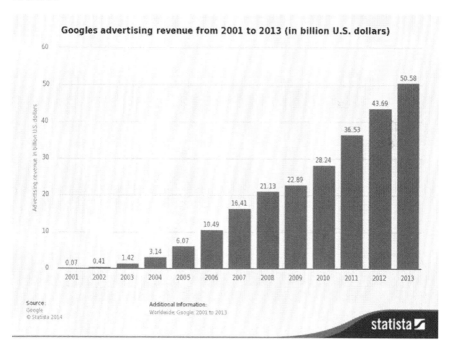

3

These numbers become even more astounding when you take into consideration the other Google properties that have been released since 2000. For instance, Android, Google's mobile operating system that has 1B+ users worldwide, doesn't even make a quarter of the revenue that AdWords does on an annual basis. Even with these numbers in Google's favor, the more impressive numbers come from the value in which businesses have gained with the platform.

As with any advertising tool, it can only grow if it is producing more revenue than it is consuming. Very few people would continue advertising if the tool they were using were not, at the very least, producing close to the same amount of money that they were putting in. It just wouldn't make financial sense for companies to continually spend money on something that wasn't producing value. To put it in context, the travel industry alone spent $750 million on AdWords in 2013 and, according to annual reports, is expecting an average return of five to fifteen times what they spent.

Not only has it helped large companies like that of the travel industry, it has helped small niche businesses reach new customers at scale. AdWords has even created entirely new job titles and an industry of advertising agencies that focus specifically on managing AdWords campaigns.

The overall value AdWords has created cannot be understated.

While ROI (Return On Investment) and average click-through-rate (CTR) has shrunken on an aggregate basis because the marketplace is now more competitive, AdWords is still an extremely valuable tool that consistently creates new customers for companies - big and small.

But how easy can it be? Well that's exactly what this book is going to address. There are a few fundamental components to AdWords that are often overlooked that can be the difference between a good campaign, and a great one.

Throughout this book we will discuss real world strategies that you can use to launch your first campaign or drastically improve an existing one. AdWords is often made out to be much more difficult than it actually is. There are some complexities, but using the strategies outlined in this book, you can attain ninety five percent of benefits within just a few hours.

What is AdWords?

Before we get into the specifics of AdWords campaigns, it is important to understand what Adwords actually is, and what it does better than any other advertising tool available today.

Let's say, for instance, you are looking for a new pair of running shoes for an upcoming 5K road race. You aren't exactly sure which brand you want, but you know that you want them to be blue - your favorite color. Without even thinking about it, you pull out your phone and start your purchasing journey by entering "best men's running shoes 2014 blue" into the ubiquitous Google search field.

No, you say? You'll ask a friend that runs marathons first. OK. But, what would you do after that?

Most likely you'd cross check what your friend said with a Google search- after all, you trust your friend, but he has been wrong before! You'd probably seek out a few reviews, perhaps read around on some forums before finally doing a bit of price comparison.

This process is repeated for every imaginable product and service, day in and day out. In fact, similar purchasing paths happen twelve billion times per month on Google. With each one of these searches comes an opportunity for businesses to match what they have for sale with customers looking to purchase exactly that - and AdWords is the tool to take advantage of that opportunity.

That's the power of AdWords, it places your advert in front of a real person (with real cash) who is actively engaged in the buying cycle.

When you look at this from Google's viewpoint, the process is simple. Every time someone searches, Google matches the most relevant advertisements to the searcher's input query. They do this by looking at a number of parameters, some set by you (the advertiser), others that are out of your control.

Often times, these 'paid' search results are more in-line with what customers are looking for than the organic results that Google determines through their search algorithm and displays underneath and along side the paid results. Once you learn how to do this, you will start seeing the most promising results from AdWords. And it's much easier than you may think.

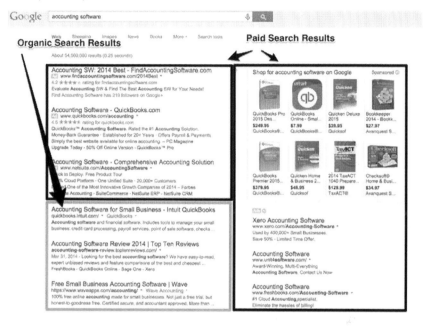

There are three main reasons why this paid search model excels.

1. Capturing Intent

In addition to the high level of scalability, AdWords' ability to precisely target searcher intent also puts it in a league of its own. What exactly does "capturing intent" mean?

Well, Google receives over one hundred billion searches per month, ranging from product research to restaurant reviews. With each one of these searches, a consumer is looking to check off an imaginary checklist of information before a purchasing event. Once you understand the fundamentals of AdWords, you can use this buying cycle to serve ads to the right person at the right time.

High intent searches like "best iPhone case for iPhone 6" are likely to result in the purchase of an iPhone case in the near future, but there will also be a lot of advertisers bidding on that term. However, searches like "pictures iPhone 6 with and without case on" will likely have less competition, but can still be valuable if used in conjunction with a great piece of content reviewing the pros and cons of using a case on your new iPhone 6+.

Each strategy has its own merits and each can work equally well. By the end of this book, you'll be able to use each to your advantage to target high intent potential customers for your business.

2. Immediacy

If you have spent any amount of time trying to rank for specific keywords in organic search results (SEO), you know that it can take a long time to start seeing results. Even the most experienced SEO professionals will tell you that three to six months is the earliest that you will see a potential uptick in traffic. And that is for traffic, not necessarily new customers.

With AdWords, you can start and pause your campaigns immediately. Even if you've never launched a campaign before, you can start targeting potential customer searches within a day or two (this is how long it normally takes Google to review ads).

Why is this important? Well, often times businesses do not have three to six months to wait around on new customers.

Using AdWords, you can start campaigns to account for yearly slow downs in sales. You can start a new campaign to launch your latest product. You can promote a Holiday sale.

Time is money, and money is the lifeblood of any business. AdWords will help you drastically cut down on the time it takes to get in front of potential customers when you need it most.

3. Scalability

The beautiful thing about this advertising medium is the scalability that you are afforded. You can spend as much or as little money as you would like based on your goals and budget.

And, AdWords offers the same toolset to all users, no matter how much they spend. If you want to spend $5 a day you will have the same available toolset as someone that is spending $1M day. While you may not have the same reach as a company with a larger budget, you can use specific strategies to find, message and sell to your potential customers.

Take this case study as an example...

John owns an auto repair shop in Orlando, FL. He has tried advertising in local print publications and has even used billboards a couple of times. Each has produced some results, but nowhere near the expectations that the sales reps selling him the advertisements had promised. John decides to spend some time learning the basics of AdWords. After a few days of studying the material, he launches his first campaign.

He understands that his business has very high 'intent' customers. Meaning, when their car has a problem, they need it fixed as soon as possible. He also understands that potential customers often do not have time to sit down at a computer, so they will probably be searching from their phone.

He launches his campaign targeting the search term "auto repair Orlando".

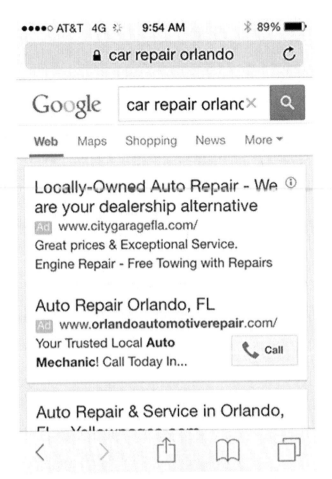

Within a week he receives eight new customers at half the cost per customer than the other ads produced.

This flexibility to adapt to any business type and customer is where the power of AdWords resides. From targeting, to budgeting and ad creation, the process has been completely democratized.

For small businesses, this has enabled them to reach more customers within a limited budget.

For large companies, it has given them the flexibility and reach to target a global audience and adjust that target from day-to-day or hour-to-hour.

So why isn't every company in the world using AdWords?

In my experience, there are three main reasons companies aren't using AdWords - all of which can be easily dispelled.

First, they've tried AdWords, spent money, and didn't get the results they expected overnight. That's normal. Results with AdWords take time. It is a process of constant gardening that rarely yields great results until the second or third month of testing. You will see *some* results immediately, as I mentioned, but to get your campaigns driving a consistent amount of profitable conversions takes time.

If you are not willing to trust the process for at least two months, you will be disappointed with AdWords as well.

The second reason that people dismiss AdWords is because they think it is 'just too complicated' for them. That couldn't be further from reality. If you are willing to put in a four hours or so of learning the fundamentals, you will be well on your way to running successful campaigns.

The last reason that I commonly hear is that companies do not have enough time to commit to managing AdWords campaigns. This is the most valid reason because time is so valuable, but let me be completely realistic about the time commitments.

The first few weeks of setting up and monitoring campaigns are the most time intensive. You can expect to spend about four hours a week. However, after everything has been smoothed out most small to medium sized business can run efficient campaigns on an hour per week or less.

Are new customers worth an hour per week? That's for you to decide. If they are, learning how to use AdWords will be well worth your time.

How AdWords Works

Before you can set up your first AdWords campaign, you must first gain an understanding of how AdWords works. In this chapter we will look at each individual component of AdWords and you will learn how it can be applied to your own advertising strategy.

A Bidding System

To describe it as simply as possible, AdWords operates on an auction system. Advertisers choose which keywords they would like to target and set the highest price they are willing to pay for a single click from that keyword (this is also know as cost-per-click or CPC). That bid is then compared to other advertisers bidding on the same keyword, in the same locations.

For example, you could pick the search phrase 'iPhone 6 case' and set a maximum bid of $1.25. This would mean that each time a potential buyer clicked on your ad, you would pay a maximum of $1.25.

However, it is important to understand that the system is a little more complex than a traditional auction. In short, Google adds an additional layer called Ad Rank, which assess the relevance of the ad to the user. This layer is added because Google wants its search users to be shown the most relevant ads possible.

If they were to have a price-only bidding system, AdWords would be filled with personal injury ads, insurance ads and other industries with the money to bid on every term imaginable. The Ad Rank system keeps competitiveness niched and allows advertisers with very specific customers to market their product effectively without having to spend exorbitant amounts of money.

Doing this retains the integrity and preciseness of their search results and keeps users happy because they are not shown unrelated ads. Google does such a good job with matching ads to user search intent that thirty six percent of its search users cannot differentiate ads from its organic search results.

That number is even more impressive when you begin to think about how long AdWords has been around. For fourteen years, Google's searchers have seen these ads on the top and on the right side of their results, but still, more than one third of them do not identify them as ads - just other possible solutions to their questions.

How Ad Rank works

Ad Rank alters the traditional idea of an auction by adding two additional components along with the bid price:

- Quality Score.
- Ad Extensions.

This means that Google compares your bid, your quality score and ad extensions to other advertisers in the auction and determines where your advert is shown.

What does it matter where they are shown?

Well, the higher on the result page, the better.

For most searches, there are two to three ads above the organic results. These three ads get the majority of the clicks for any given search.

There are exceptions, but the top three results are where you want your ads to be. Keeping an Average Position (a metric you can track in the AdWords dashboard) in the two-to-three range is a general best practice and will likely yield much better results than an average position of four and below.

The Bid

The bid component of the Ad Rank equation is pretty straightforward, but in practice, can become one of the most complex.

Companies must take into consideration how much to bid on keywords based on their product's profit margins, targeted acquisition cost and conversion rate. If you end up bidding a random number, you could end up paying more for a new customer than they are worth.

The simplest way to land on a reasonable bid is to find your average breakeven point for a new customer. To find this, just multiply your current conversion rate, which can be found in Google Analytics, by how much a new customer is worth.

It is important to understand how much each new customer is worth, on average. This is also called Lifetime Value (LTV) and it takes into account how much a new customer is going to spend over the entire relationship with your product or service.

For instance, a customer may only spend $50 on the first purchase to your site, but may come back on four more occasions and spend a total of $650. Their Lifetime Value would be $700.

Back to the breakeven point. If you have a five percent conversion rate, meaning you get one out of every twenty new visitors to make a purchase or contact you (this depends on what you are considering a 'conversion', it will differ for each business), and the average Lifetime Value of a new customers is $50, the highest you would want to initially bid would be $2.50.

Conversion Rate x Lifetime Value = Suggested Starting Bid
0.05 x $50 = $2.50

After running your campaign for a few weeks, you may determine that traffic from AdWords converts at a higher rate than other traffic sources. This gives you the opportunity to increase your bids.

When setting up your ads, you select the price you want to pay. The default bid can be determined on the campaign, Ad Group or individual keyword level.

Quality Score

Quality Score is Google's algorithm that approximates how likely your ad is to be clicked on when displayed in the search results that you are targeting. Google scores this on a scale of one to ten - one being the worst possible score and ten being the best.

The metric takes several points into consideration, but all you have to do to really understand how to maximize your quality score is remember one thing- *be specific*. If you are targeting the keyword "men's running shoes for marathons blue", make sure that your ads talk about the same theme. Your landing page, or the page that users who click your ad get sent to, should certainly be a page containing blue running shoes for men that can be worn for marathons or a very close derivative.

This seems like a no-brainer, but failing to do this is one of the biggest pitfalls in AdWords campaigns.

The best approach for this is to think like a consumer. What would you expect to see, given the searches you are targeting? Remember the click term much match the landing page.

Ad Extensions

Ad Extensions are the third component of Ad Rank. We will get into how to get the most out of these later in the book, but for now, just know that these extensions add more context and content to your ads. The more extensions you can add to your campaigns, the higher your quality score will be.

You've probably seen Ad Extensions before, but just didn't know what they were. An example of an Ad Extension is the 'call' button that you often see on mobile searches. That button can be added through a campaign and lets customers one-touch dial a provided number directly from the advertisement.

Another one that you may have seen is sitelinks. The additional links are usually below the main text and allow users to click into more specific pages on a site. This can improve conversions rates because users can get to the pages they are looking for more quickly.

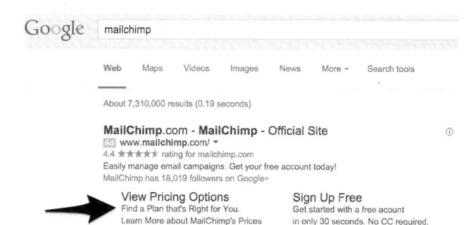

There are many more Ad Extensions that you can use in your campaigns. Each provides a unique opportunity to improve the click rate of your ads and improve your Ad Rank.

The available Ad Extensions change fairly frequently, but as I am writing this the ones currently ready for use are:

- Sitelink extensions
- Location extensions
- Call extensions
- App extensions
- Review extensions
- Callout extensions

Bringing Them All Together...

Bids, Quality Score and Ad Extensions together are calculated to get your Ad Rank. However, not all three are weighted the same. Quality Score is far and away the most important component of the equation.

Your exact Ad Rank number is not as easy to calculate, especially after the addition of Ad Extensions into the formula, but you can still understand the basic formula by multiplying your Quality Score by your bid.

The higher your Quality Score, the less you will have to spend on the same keywords. A Quality Score of 5 is Google's benchmark, meaning that it is the average quality score. This chart below details how an increase and decrease in Quality Score can affect how much you spend on a given ad.

Quality Score	Effect on Cost Per Click (CPC)
10	Discounted by 50%
9	Discounted by 44.2%
8	Discounted by 37.50%
7	Discounted by 28.60%
6	Increased by 16.70%
5	Google's Benchmark
4	Increased by 25%
3	Increased by 67.30%
2	Increased by 150.00%
1	Increased by 400%

Using the numbers from the chart above and a base bid of $2, an advertiser with a Quality Score of 10 would pay just $1, whereas an advertiser with a Quality Score of 3 would pay $3.32.

While that may not seem like a huge deal for one click, when you are getting thousands of clicks per month, it starts to add up. For instance, with a Quality Score of 10 and a monthly budget of a $1,000, you would receive 1,000 clicks to your site. With the same budget and a Quality Score of 3, you would receive just 299 clicks.

The key lesson from this chapter is to understand how Google ranks advertisers and how you can use their calculations to improve your campaigns to get more clicks for less money. If you focus on being as precise and specific with your keywords, text ads, and landing pages as you can, you will be head and shoulders above most advertisers using AdWords today.

The Blueprint

Many companies and marketers lose money with AdWords. Not because they aren't smart or don't know who their customers are, but because they don't know how to properly wield AdWords as a marketing tool to do their work for them.

This blueprint will walk you through the eight steps that, if done correctly, can guarantee successful campaigns - and not just successful for a month or two, but for the long term. I have personally seen this work for hundreds of companies across several different industries.

These steps are not groundbreaking alone, but used in conjunction with one another, they can produce consistent results that can help you build more leads, sell more products, and expand your business.

1. Account and Campaign Structure

2. Location, Location, Location

3. Bidding and Budgeting

4. Ad Extensions

5. Writing Ads

6. Keywords and Match Types

7. Research

8. Optimizing and Testing

We will now look at each of these steps in turn, starting with your account.

Step 1: Account and Campaign Structure

The first step to running a successful AdWords account is the set up. Before you add a single keyword or write your first ad, it is extremely important to have your campaign set up correctly, or in a way that facilitates ongoing success.

Not only does it help with organization and constant optimization, a thoughtfully composed account can enable higher Quality Scores and click-through rates, which will ultimately determine if your campaigns are successful or not.

Your Account

Your account is the top level of AdWords. It is where all of your payment information and settings are housed.

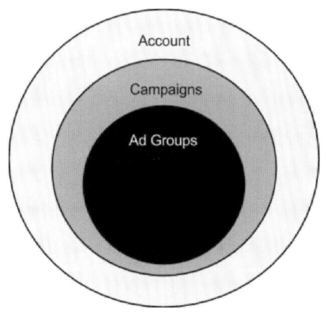

If you are managing multiple companies' AdWords campaigns, I would suggest creating a separate account for each. Or, if you are being hired to work on an already existing account, just ask that account owner to give you access. You can do this by going to the **Account Settings** link in the **Settings** drop down menu on the top of the AdWords interface.

Next, just ask to be added as a user using your email address.

Jamming multiple campaigns for different websites into one account can cause confusion and lead to poorly managed campaigns. It is best to keep things separate whenever possible.

Google has another solution for users managing multiple campaigns, called My Client Center (MCC). It is a really helpful tool if you are in that situation.

For the majority of users, however, one account will be enough as you will likely be managing AdWords for one business.

While most features in the AdWords account are self explanatory, such as billing and notification settings, one feature is often overlooked and can help save a lot of time solving problems.

Let's say, for instance, you and another co-worker, Joe, share access to an AdWords account for your taco restaurant. You check on your campaigns on Monday, like you always do. Only this time, you notice something alarming. You've received half the amount of clicks that you normally receive and a quarter of the normal conversions!

Panic sets in. You've made no changes to the account. You start clicking into all of your campaigns to see where the issue could be, but that is like trying to find a needle in a haystack.

Luckily, there is an account feature to easily help you solve this conundrum. In the **Tools** tab, you can click **'Change History'** to see every change that's been made to the account and by whom. You see that your co-worker, Joe, paused your best performing keyword for some unknown reason. Joe's an idiot.

From there, you just unpause the keyword. Problem solved. Time for a friendly word with Joe.

The thing to keep in mind in regards to your Account is that it is the home base. It is the top level for everything that goes on with AdWords.

Campaigns

Campaigns are usually a first stumbling block for users initially setting up AdWords. It can be hard to grasp what deserves to be a Campaign and what should be an Ad Group - a lower level in the hierarchy.

Think about Campaigns as a folder inside your AdWords account. They hold information about targeting, default bids and performance of the Ad Groups within them. And like a folder, it is beneficial to keep the contents inside of them themed and organized.

Ad Groups, on the other hand, are the single files inside of that folder. They hold detailed performance metrics about their Ad Group only.

So, you'll want to create a campaign for each product or service that you are marketing. Each Ad Group should be a variation of the product or service, or alternative names for that product or service. An example of alternative names would be purse and handbag. Both would be in the same Campaigns, but you would create one Ad Group for 'purse' and one Ad Group for 'handbag'

If you have decided you want to advertise your company as a whole, you will want to create a campaign for that, as well.

Let's say, for instance, you own TY Power Tools. Over the last few years, TY has built a reputation as the premiere e-commerce power tools website in the southwest United States. You originally built the business from word-of-mouth advertising, but have decided it is time to ramp up your advertising using AdWords. You want to advertise to potential customers that are looking for a reputable place to buy many different power tools and equipment, as well as individual products.

You would start by creating a **campaign** for "power tools online" that would highlight your great selection of power tools. You would also create a campaign for each specific product that you want to advertise, which are your Hitachi miter saw and Blue Clean pressure washer.

Another campaign type that you can use is categories. This is especially useful if you are an online retailer with hundreds or thousands of products.

Using PPC power tools again as an example, a campaign for "miter saw" would be justified if they sold additional brands of miter saws other than the Hitachi. Even "Hitachi miter saws" could be a campaign if they were selling multiple models within that brand name.

The last type of campaign that you know about and use EVERY SINGLE TIME is branded campaigns, or a campaign that shows ads to users searching for your company's name. So, anytime someone searches for TY Power Tools, or a close variant, your ad will show up at the top of the results page.

Now, it may seem counterintuitive to have a campaign for your company's name, and you may be asking, "Won't users already be able to find me through organic search?" Yes, they will, but a branded campaign has a few benefits that you cannot ignore.

First, it is like having a top search result that you can change or edit at anytime. You can adjust the messaging for seasonality. You can promote a special that you are running and you can send visitors to unique landing pages that have higher conversion rates than your homepage. Also, you can have an Ad Extension that can convert potential users on the spot, such as call extensions, and use direct links to profitable landing pages with sitelinks.

Branded campaigns will also likely be your most inexpensive CPC because you own the branded term. No one else will be sending traffic from a 'TY Power Tools' search to the TY Power Tools website. Even if competitors do bid for your branded terms (sometimes they will), they will be paying much more for a click than you because your Quality Score will be substantially higher and your ad will almost always be in a higher position that theirs

While these types of campaign formats serve as a general rule for starting out, there are certainly exceptions. As you get more familiar with AdWords and your campaigns, you may find that other organizational structures work better for you. And that's fine. Performance is the main goal.

The last tip regarding campaigns is about the campaign set up. When creating your Campaigns, use **Search Network Only** campaigns with **All Features** enabled. While the other campaign types provide opportunity, **Search Network Only** will produce the most consistent results. Including **Display Network** in your campaign increases your ads impressions, but nearly always drives click-through-rates lower because they display ads on websites, not search results. One of the main benefits of AdWords is capturing user intent based on what that user has searched; including the Display Network does not take advantage of this benefit. Google simply scans the content of the pages using AdSense, and if it is related to keywords in your Campaign, will serve your ads to the users on that page. Users reading a blog don't have the same intent as a user searching for a product.

This is the best place to start as a beginner. Even now, this campaign set up yields eighty percent of my ongoing campaign results.

Ad Groups

Ad Groups are a set of keywords, ads, and bids you manage together in order to show ads to people likely to be interested in them.Ad Groups live inside of campaigns, as I've mentioned. You can have multiple Ad Groups inside each campaign.

The way to think about Ad Groups is as adjectives, or alternate descriptions of your campaign's main theme. They provide a way to thematically group similar keywords and ads together. And because being as *specific* as possible is always the goal, there should rarely be more than five to ten keywords in any given Ad Group.

A good example of this would be if you sold guitar and piano lessons online.

"Guitar" and "piano" would likely be your two campaigns, as these are the two services you are advertising. As we talked about in the previous section, this grouping will allow you to easily compare performance and make adjustments where needed.

Potential customers may use many different phrases to describe what you are selling, therefore, you would want to create multiple Ad Groups for each campaign.

This is an example of how your account structure could look:

Piano (Campaign)
Piano Lessons Online (Ad Group)
Piano Tutorials Online (Ad Group)
Piano Video Course (Ad Group)
Guitar (Campaign)
Guitar Lessons Online (Ad Group)
Guitar Tutorial Online (Ad Group)
Guitar Video Course (Ad Group)

This is just an example, and there may be many other Ad Groups inside each campaign.

For each of those Ad Groups, there should be very close derivatives of that description. For instance, keywords inside of the 'Piano Lessons Online' Ad Group could include 'best piano lessons online', 'piano lessons online', 'piano lessons online with video', 'piano lessons online for beginners', and 'piano lessons online for dummies'.

We will cover keywords in a later chapter, but just know that this will help improve your Quality Score.

Following this outline for your account's structure will put you on the path to success. Feel free to experiment with different structures that fit your needs. After you are more familiar with AdWords as a whole, your account may look very different than what I have outlined...or maybe it will look exactly the same.

Review

1. **Account > Campaign > Ad Groups**

2. Campaigns should be specific to a product, service or category.

3. Ad Groups should be different ways to describe the campaign's main idea.

4. No more than five to ten keyword in each Ad Group to start.

Step 2: Location, Location, Location

When setting up campaigns, location targeting can often be an afterthought. The default setting (for those in the U.S.) is to target the United States and Canada and that is where many campaigns stay for their entirety.

Location targeting should be viewed as an opportunity to test and capitalize on your best performing geographic areas - especially if you have a limited budget. You'll want to target the areas that consistently perform the best for you. Conversion rate, average order value, and revenue are the primary metrics to use when deciding this.

For this example, let's imagine that you run a computer programming conference in Miami, FL, each January. You expect some return attendees from last year's event, but will have to get at least 500 new attendees to sign up to make the event a success.

You decide to use AdWords as the primary tool to get you to that goal. You then start running a campaign targeting techies in the United States. After a few days, you notice that your conversion rate is hovering around one percent. Worried that conversion rates like that are going to cost you more money than they are going to make you, you decide to make a switch.

You then remember a stat from last year's group of attendees - forty percent of them came from a handful of cities. You switch your location targeting to only serve ads to users in New York City, San Francisco, Chicago, Austin and Atlanta. Within two days, your conversion rate jumps to five percent and you're back on track to meet your goal.

While this is just an example, I've seen small tweaks to location targeting yield similar results. Google Analytics is a great source for finding historical data like this.

Using the **Geo Report** in Google Analytics, you can view engagement statistics, such as average time on site and average number of pages viewed. You can also chip away at the data all the way down to metro area, which is helpful for precise targeting.

In certain instances, separate campaigns for each targeted location are necessary. If you sell products that vary heavily on seasonality and/or weather, you will most likely not serve the same ads to searchers in Florida that you would to those in Oregon.

It would be advantageous for an e-commerce store that sells fishing rods to have a campaign for "ice fishing" that targets cold weather climates in the winter, and a campaign that features standard, year-around equipment to warm and moderate climates where "ice fishing" would not be applicable.

For restaurants and other brick-and-mortar retailers that have several locations, creating one campaign with multiple targets can work. If the product is generally undifferentiated from location to location, there is no need to create multiple campaigns.

Selecting the targeting radius for local campaigns is not an exact science and can differ from business-to-business. Some high-demand restaurants may bring customers from twenty miles away or more and can warrant a targeting radius that supports this demand.

On the other hand, some stores may only draw customers from a very close proximity; let's say five miles away. The best way to gauge this is to ask current customers. Each time a current customer is from outside your targeting radius, consider expanding it. A good starting point is a ten mile radius and then adjust from there, based on performance and anecdotal evidence.

Language Targeting

Language targeting and location targeting are closely related. When selecting a location, Google will give you a notification in your account detailing which languages are significantly represented in that area. For instance, when targeting Canada, French is regularly suggested for language targeting.

Targeting different languages can be an easy win, but it is not without its own unique challenges. The biggest thing to keep in mind when thinking about targeting multiple languages is that **AdWords does not translate ads.** You must translate them into the language of your choice and create separate campaigns for each language that you are targeting.

If you are interested in translating ads and do not speak the language that you would like to target, head over to oDesk or Elance. They both have large quantities of freelancers that are native speakers in most languages. The rates are reasonable and I have personally had great results using both services.

Another thing to keep in mind is user experience. Once someone clicks on an ad, will your site be translated?

Google Translate has plugins for CMS's like Wordpress, but its output can often be lost in translation. Sometimes 'close enough' works, but if you think that a certain language could produce bigger results, it may be worth translating your entire site. It seems like a lot of work, but most of the time, your competitors will not spend the time and money to do this.

Review

1. Understand what geographic regions your best customers come from.

2. Create campaigns for each location when necessary.

3. Account for seasonality and weather.

4. Create separate campaigns for language targeting.

5. Be sure to translate ads for each language targeted.

Step 3: Bidding and Budgeting

The easiest way to decide where to set your default bid when starting out is to calculate your conversion rate times the profit margin of the product or service that you are advertising. This formula will get you to a point where you are breaking even with your campaign.

Conversion Rate x Per Unit Profit = Breakeven CPC

Example: TY Power Tools wants to start advertising for one of their new products, a Black & Decker drill. Through their Google Analytics account they see that the product page for that drill has a ten-percent conversion rate and they know they make $30 profit from each unit sold. Using the formula above, their breakeven CPC would be three dollars.

10% Coversion Rate x $30 Per Unit Profit = $3 Breakeven CPC

This formula is a good starting point, but breakeven should not be your end goal. Even though once you get a new customer, the likelihood of them buying from you again drastically increases (assuming you meet their expectations), you should try to drive down your average CPC to increase your campaign's profitability. There are several other options that you can use to increase the effectiveness.

The first way is to always manually select bids. Google provides an option to automatically adjust your bid to increase its position, but this reduces the amount of flexibility you have and removes some of the human ingenuity that you can leverage when managing your campaign.

You can set your default bids by campaign or Ad Group, but once you start getting data in after a campaign has been running for a while, the best way to approach setting bids is based on keyword level.

You will begin to see the conversion rates for each keyword and can adjust your bids to reflect the breakeven CPC. So, if the keyword 'best Black and Decker drill' has a twenty percent conversion rate, you could double that keyword's max CPC bid to $6.

20% Conversion Rate x $30 Per Unit Profit = $6 Breakeven CPC

One of the most efficient way to control your spending and CPA (cost per acquisition) is to use **Enhanced CPC**. This option uses your historical conversion data to bid keywords up or down based on the keyword's likelihood to convert. To enable this, you will have to have **Conversion Tracking** on. This can be done either by setting it up through AdWords or connecting your Google Analytics account to your AdWords account. Both are fairly simple and should not take much time to implement.

Once that is set up and you have received a few conversions, Google will notify you of which campaigns are eligible to use Enhanced CPC. Once enabled, Google will begin the optimization process. For keywords that are more likely to result in a sale, they will adjust your current bid by up to thirty percent.

From my experience, this bidding feature can increase your conversion with less clicks in a matter of hours. It is always best to monitor the change for a few days after implementing, but results are usually favorable.

The last option that you have for setting your bids is called **Focus on Conversions** or **Conversion Optimizer**. What this does is focus on optimizing your bid to reach a CPA that you set. This is different from the other models that focus strictly on CPC.

This is a great option for advertisers that have a strict threshold they need to meet to make a profit. Google will use your data to bid keywords up or down, adjust targeting, and manipulate other targeting options to find the sweet spot for your campaigns.

To enable this option, you will have to have **Conversion-Tracking** setup and you will also have to have had at least fifteen conversions within the last thirty days. Google will alert you once your campaigns have reached that threshold with this option, as well, and will then allow you to switch over your bidding options.

While Conversion Optimizer may be a good solution for some, I've had more success with Enhanced CPC.

Budgeting

One mistake that happens quite frequently is setting a budget so low that there is virtually no way for you to test your campaigns. A good rule of thumb is to set your monthly budget to a point where you can garner at least 500 clicks but 1,000 clicks per month is ideal.

With 500 clicks, you should see a few conversions and start to see which campaigns are performing best. As you begin to optimize your campaigns, you should see the CPA drop and quantity of conversions go up.

Another thing to note is that AdWords makes you choose your budget on a daily basis. However, most businesses operate on monthly budgets.

The quickest way to work out the math is to simply divide your monthly budget by 30.4 (average number of days in a month).

$1,000 monthly budget / 30.4 = $32.80 per day

Google will often go over your daily budget - sometimes by up to twenty percent. However, as long as your budget remains consistent, it will never exceed your daily budget times 30.4 in a month.

The reason they do this is to account for seasonality and unforeseen upticks and ensure you do not miss out on potential increases in conversions.

Review

1. Understand your breakeven point.

2. Always manually select keywords.

3. Use Enhanced CPC when available, but test Conversion Optimizer.

4. Start with a budget that gives your campaigns a chance to succeed.

Step 4: Ad Extensions

We have already discussed the importance of Ad Extensions in respect to Ad Rank. While the effects are still hard to directly quantify and calculate, Google has clearly made an effort to communicate that Ad Extensions *do affect* the ranking of your ads and campaigns. This point alone should be enough motivation for you to use Ad Extensions in your campaigns, but there are even more benefits to discuss, if you need further convincing.

The first benefit is that Ad Extensions provide alternate actions for your advertisements. Clicking on your ad's main link will almost always be the primary action, but Ad Extensions provide other ways for users to interact with your ads based on their intent.

They provide a way to go to alternative pages on your website, download mobile apps, see reviews and even call your business directly from the ad. Providing these actions lets potential customers convert in a way that is most comfortable to them. They also make your ad bulkier, which draws in people's attention when viewing the results page.

The best part about Ad Extensions is that optimizing them to improve Ad Rank is quite simple. All you have to do is use as many of them in your campaigns as possible. The more you use that are applicable to your business, the better. Additionally, you should be able to recognize which are applicable without much thought. For instance, if you do not have a mobile app, you are obviously not going to be able to use **App Download** extensions.

Over the last few years, Google has consistently tested new Ad Extensions and released the successful ones to all accounts. To stay abreast to the latest changes and additions, make sure you have your **New Features** enabled in **Notification Preferences**. This way, you will be able to add new Ad Extensions the day they come out, if your account is eligible.

Even with all of the additions to the Ad Extension lineup, there have been a few that have remained consistent - both in availability and performance.

Sitelinks are the consummate Ad Extension and they are extensions that every single campaign on AdWords should be using. Essentially, sitelinks provide alternative links that can send users to pages within your site other than your ad's main destination page.

Zappos always does a tremendous job with AdWords. This is an example of how they use sitelinks for the branded search "Zappos":

Zappos.com - Zappos - Official Site
www.zappos.com/ ▾
Fast & Free Shipping On All Orders. Shop Shoes, Clothes, Boots & More!
Zappos.com has 121,303 followers on Google+

Women's Shoes	Women's Clothing
Men's Shoes	Sandals
Kids Shoes	Men's Clothing

Alternatively, this example is how Zappos approaches sitelinks for the more specific search "Zappos women's shoes":

Zappos.com - Women's Shoes at Zappos
www.zappos.com/Womens-Shoes ▾
Fast, Free Shipping & Returns, 365 Day Returns on Women's Shoes
Zappos.com has 141,665 followers on Google+

Women's Boots	Espadrilles
Women's Flats	Gladiator Sandals
Women's Dress Shoes	Heels

As you can see, they employ very different strategies for each search. With each strategy, they are essentially getting six ads for the price of one. They are communicating with customers that they have shoes in all of the categories listed, which will likely result in higher click-through rates.

The question you should be asking yourself each time you add an Ad Extension to a campaign is, "What else would a customer searching for this be interested in?"

Often times, the answer to that question is a closely related product or additional product categories. You can drill down one level in the category hierarchy or go horizontally.

An example of drilling down for the search "men's running shoes" would be including categories such as "Nike running shoes", "Adidas running shoes" and "Asics running shoes".

An example of using horizontal categories for sitelinks for the search "men's running shoes" would be including "men's cross trainers", "men's barefoot shoes", and "men's workout shoes".

Both strategies can work. It is just a matter of testing to see which strategy works for your products.

Another way to approach sitelinks is to include your most highly valued pages. For an e-commerce store, this may be the page that contains your best-selling or highest-grossing product. For a company that provides a service, this could be your 'Contact' and/or 'About' pages.

If you are using Google Analytics, there is an easy way to determine which page(s) is your most highly valued. Google provides a metric called **Page Value**.

Page value is calculated by dividing the value of a conversion across every page that was visited by that user. It is not a perfect metric, but it can certainly point you in the direction of your most important pages.

The second of the two most important Ad Extensions is the **Call Extension**. If you run campaigns for a local company or a service-based company, this can drive a high percentage of your conversions. Call Extensions include your phone number in your ads to allow customers to inquire about your business or place an order. The other benefit of this extension is that Google provides you the option of using a tracking number, which is helpful for quantifying conversions.

The tracking numbers just forward calls from the tracking number to the number that you provided. This is how Google tracks the quantity of calls, how long calls last and where the calls are from. You can then use this data to optimize your campaigns.

For example, let's assume you know that calls lasting less than thirty seconds are very rarely from customers. They are mostly misdialed calls or quick inquiries. You can use that information to change the setting in your campaign to only count calls over thirty seconds as a conversion.

Another thing to note is that Call Extensions look and perform differently in mobile searches than they do in desktop searches,

From my experience, the mobile version of Call Extensions performs better for high intent searches related to local business. The desktop version performs well, but may result in more support or question-based calls.

If you are seeing certain campaigns or Ad Groups produce more question-based calls, you may want to pause Call Extensions. You may not want to be paying money to answer customer questions. Allowing them to click through to your website and find the answer themselves may be sufficient.

Restaurants and local service companies, such as pest control, stand to benefit the most from the mobile extension. It gives people who are ready to make a decision an easy way to complete that process. If you are in either of these types of business, you know that calls have a much better conversion rate than a website visit.

Call Extensions and sitelinks are the two crown jewels of the Ad Extension universe, but you should still experiment with others. Always test out new extensions when they are released, even if you think they have a small chance of being successful. You just might be surprised by the results.

Review

1. Use as many applicable sitelinks as you can.

2. Sitelinks provide more conversion opportunities.

3. Call Extensions work well, but be aware of high customer-question calls.

4. Sign up for AdWords announcement emails.

5. Test new extensions as they become available.

Step 5: Writing Ads

We are now moving onto the process of actually writing your advertisements. Bet you didn't think it would take this long to get here, did you?

The ads are the most customer-facing element of the campaign, but in actuality, they only make up a small percentage of the whole. Nonetheless, there is still a lot to cover and there are several things to keep in mind when writing your ads.

First, it is important to understand the three main components of AdWords text ads.

1. The Headline

The headline is allowed to have up to twenty five characters and it is the most noticeable element of the ad. It is blue and the font size is larger than that of the other components.

When writing the headline, the goal is to try to catch potential customers' attention. Most likely, the perfect headline combination will come from testing and reiterating your ad copy, but attention-grabbing headlines can use a number of different styles. They can be a question, an exact match of a search, or a bold claim, but you do not want to have the exact same wording as all of the other ads in a search.

Be different. Be unique. Try to empathize with the customer and understand their mindset.

If you are selling a product, think about what problem your product is solving for a customer. Use that in the ads.

If we go back to the running shoes example, there are various reasons why someone could be looking for new running shoes. Highlighting a major problem, like shin splints, could win clicks over ads that just say 'Running Shoes for Sale'.

'Tired of Shin Splints?'

Don't get me wrong, generic ads can work but, more often than not, in competitive searches, ads that blend in with the rest of the results have a lower click rate than those that stand out.

Using unique headlines is also great ammunition for smaller companies that are competing with behemoths.

Because companies like Zappos are running so many campaigns, they often have to write ads programmatically. This means they use their product names to determine ad copy so that they do not have to write each ad individually for their hundreds of thousands of products. Doing this saves time, but also cuts down on creativity. Use this to your advantage and be different.

2. Description Lines

The description lines are two lines of text that are displayed underneath the headline. They are afforded up to thirty five characters each.

Most of the time, these lines are used to answer the 'What?' and 'Why?' once you have captured a user's attention with your headline. This is your chance to intrigue them enough to click through to your website.

If you have a clear differentiator compared to your competitors, use it here. Words like "highest rated" or "best [insert product here]" are great to use. Also, if you have a special promotion or an offer, such as free shipping, your description line is a great place to test it.

If you have the room and wordsmithery to fit a differentiator and an added bonus, these generally work best.

Side ad

Tired of Shin Splints?
www.runningshoes.com/womens
Best Rated Women's Running Shoes.
Free Shipping on Orders Over $40.

Top ad

Tired of Shin Splints? - Best Rated Women's Running Shoes.
www.runningshoes.com/womens
Free Shipping on Orders Over $40.

Another thing to keep in mind is that if you have the keywords that a user searched for in your description lines, they will be bolded. This can draw more attention to your ads, but you do not want to use unnatural or poorly styled sentences just in the name of getting key phrases bolded.

The last thing to note about the description lines is that punctuation matters.

If you end the first description line with a period, it will insert a line break and push the second description line down.

If you do not insert a period, it will be one complete line if the ad shows up in the top results.

Women's Running Shoes
www.runningshoes.com/womens
Check out the best selection of
marathon running shoes online.

Women's Running Shoes
www.runningshoes.com/womens
Check out the best selection of marathon running shoes online.

When you are creating your ad, AdWords provides you with a preview tool that will show you exactly how that ad will be displayed based on its position.

3. The URLs

The last two elements of ad writing are related to URLs.

The URL is your website address. The display URL is the visual element that users see in your ads. This is allowed to be up to thirty five characters.

The destination URL is where they are sent, also known as a landing page. Google does police this function to make sure there is not any trickery from advertisers. It is not uncommon for the actual URL on your site to be long and ugly. Often times, there are long strings or UTM codes appended to the URL that can clutter up search results. Google allows you to display one URL (e.g. yoursite.com) but actually have a different destination URL (e.g. yoursite.com?campaign=adwords) The main reason they have the display URL is to provide a 'pretty version' of a URL. The best practice for the display URL is to use an easily read version of your URL, if possible. Make potential customers feel safe about what they are clicking on.

The destination URL should be fairly self-explanatory - send users to the page on your website that best matches their search.

This is why being as *specific* and *precise* as possible with your Ad Groups is so important. If your Ad Group is showing up for a bunch of different searches using different terminology, it can be difficult to write ads. The more specific your Ad Groups are, the better you can write ads that resonate with customers.

Before we end this chapter, I want to introduce an advanced topic called **dynamic keyword insertion**. What this does is insert the phrase that a user searched into your advertisement copy.

If you have "red running shoes" as a keyword in your campaign *and* you are using dynamic keyword insertion, AdWords inserts that keyword phrase wherever dynamic keyword insertion is used.

Side ad

{KeyWord:Red Running Shoes}
www.runningshoes.com/{keyword:red-shoes}
Check out the best selection of
{keyword:red running shoes} online.

Top ad

{KeyWord:Red Running Shoes}
www.runningshoes.com/{keyword:red-shoes}
Check out the best selection of {keyword:red running shoes} online.

If the phrase searched is longer than the permitted number of characters, AdWords will use your backup text, which is the phrase directly following the colon.

Dynamic keyword insertion can be used in the headline, description lines, or display URL, and can make your ads seem more relevant to users. It is important, however, to understand exactly what phrases are triggering ads. Not being aware of this can lead to less than optimal traffic and performance.

To read more about dynamic keyword insertion, follow this link to the AdWords Learning Center.

Review

1. Be unique.

2. Highlight what makes you different.

3. Use a descriptive display URL.

4. Experiment with dynamic keyword insertion ads.

Step 6: Keywords and Match Types

Keywords are the searches that people make using Google that you would like to target with your ads. They are the heart of your AdWords campaigns. They are what make everything else come together. They determine which searches your text ads are triggered for and which they are not. We have continuously discussed specificity. That idea should be the sole goal when adding keywords to your Ad Groups and campaigns.

There are a few different ways to target user searches with keywords. These are called **match types**.

The match types tell AdWords which words should be included in a search to trigger your ad, what order those words should be in, and whether or not additional words can be added on to the phrase you are targeting.

Below are the five match type options:

1. Broad Match

Broad match affords the most search-matching flexibility of all of the match types. It gives Google the ability to change out words for close synonyms and add prefixes and suffixes onto your keywords.

Example:

Your Keywords: women's running shoes

Possible Search Triggers: ladies jogging shoes, best selection of women's running shoes, buy ladies running shoes online, where to buy ladies running shoes in Orlando, FL

Now, your keyword would still be available to be triggered for "women's running shoes", but it opens up the possibilities for more potential searches, which can be dangerous. Opening up matches like this could cause your ads to be triggered for erroneous or non-profitable searches.

The benefit of this match type is that there are more potential searches for your keyword to show up. This can be helpful for categories with low search volume.

However, this matching option can teeter your ads on the brink of irrelevance with certain searches. I very rarely advise using this type of matching, but if you are having a tough time getting the number of impressions and/or clicks that you need for your budget, it could be worth experimenting.

2. Broad Match Modifier

Broad match modifier is my personal favorite and my most used keywords match type. I find that it seems to combine the positive aspects of each match type into one easy-to-use option. It provides some of the flexibility and increased impressions of broad match, while still being precise when needed, like exact match, which we will cover shortly.

To put it in plain English, broad modifier is saying, "These words have to be included exactly how I have typed them, but can be in any order and other words can be searched with it."

The syntax for using broad modifier is to add a plus sign in front of the words that need to be included in a user's search (+keyword +keyword +keyword).

Example:

Your Keyword: +women's +running +shoes

Possible Search Triggers: best women's running shoes, buy women's running shoes online, highest rated women's running shoes

The more words you include in your keyword, the more specific this match type can be. The reason this match type can be so efficient is because over sixty percent of searches have never been searched for before. It is difficult, and sometimes impossible, to think of all the combinations and variants that a person can search. Broad modifier allows you to set a hierarchy of keywords that have to be included and allows for variations on other descriptors.

3. Phrase Match

Phrase match is a cousin of modified broad match, but adds an additional requirement layer. It says, "I want these words included, in this order, but additional words can be added in front or behind the phrase".

The syntax for using phrase match is to put quotes around your keywords ("keywords").

Example:

Your Keyword: "women's running shoes"

Possible Search Triggers: buy women's running shoes online, women's running shoes sale orlando, what are the highest rated women's running shoes.

As the example above shows, it is important to understand the searcher's intent. If you are selling women's running shoes online, you probably do not want to show your ads to people searching for local sales.

Phrase match is helpful to use when you are in a technical industry or an industry where different word orders can hold completely different meanings.

4. Exact Match

Exact match is exactly what it sounds like. It is a way of telling AdWords, "I want these exact keywords to be searched for, in this exact order. Nothing added, nothing removed."

The syntax for using exact match is to wrap your keywords or phrases in square brackets ([keywords]).

Example:

Your Keywords: [women's running shoes]

Possible Search Triggers: women's running shoes

Obviously, using this match type will drastically reduce the number of searches that your ads will be triggered for. However, there are a few cases where this is helpful. One case is if you have found specific keywords that have a lot of search volume and you have a high conversion rate for them. An example of this would be a product with a model number. Something like [red Nike air max 90 hyperfuse] would result in a high intent user that you could send to that product page.

Another case would be for branded search campaigns. If you own Johnny's Shoe Emporium, you can use exact match to target those keywords ([Johnny's Shoe Emporium])and show ads highlighting your current specials, your locations, and your inventory to potential customers.

5. Negative Match

The last match type is called negative match. This is saying to AdWords, "I do not want any searches with this word to trigger my ads".

Using negative keywords is one of the most overlooked components of a successful AdWords campaign. If you do not have a grasp on exactly what is triggering your ads, you will be spending money on low converting clicks and, sometimes, searches that are completely unrelated to your product or service.

The syntax for adding negative keywords is adding a minus in front of a keyword (-keyword -keyword -keyword).

Example:

Your Keyword: -ebay

The example above would be a way to reduce some of the impressions for your targeted search of "**+women's +running +shoes**" from customers that are clearly looking for products from a particular retailer.

Another use of negative match is for budget control. If you have determined that a particular word indicates that a user is still doing initial research, you may want to add that as a negative keyword.

Searches like "what running shoes sponsor Gisele Bundchen", are probably many steps away from purchase, whereas a search containing an exact color and model of a shoe generally indicates higher intent.

There are a few ways to find negative keywords. One way is by using a preexisting list of popular negative keywords. They are widely available and can be found with a simple Google search. These lists provide words that are low converting. For example, the keyword "jobs" is often used as a negative keyword for companies advertising services. Unless you are advertising a lawn care job opening, you do not want "lawn care jobs Atlanta" to be triggering your ads meant to attract new customers.

Another way to find negative keywords is to let your campaigns run for a few weeks, then analyze the keywords that have triggered your ads. By going to **Keyword** > **Details** > **Search Term** > **All** and viewing the generated report in AdWords, you can see the keywords that triggered ads and delete the ones that you do not think are beneficial.

It is a best practice to do this at least once per month. There is a very low chance that you are going to be able to guess all of the toxic keywords when first launching your campaign. You will be surprised at some of the searches that triggered your ads when you view your keyword report.

Review

1. Understand your matching options.

2. Understand searcher intent.

3. Always include negative keywords.

Step 7: Research

Research is another aspect of AdWords campaigns that is often overlooked. Advertisers think that they intuitively 'know' what their customers put into the search field when looking for their products or services - but very rarely are they correct.

As we discussed in the previous lesson, there are hundreds or even thousands of possible variations and descriptions for the same product. It is not possible to predict what each of those searches will be. Also, when you do try to select keywords and targeting groups for your campaigns, you will often select the most obvious. These may have the most search volume, but will also have the highest competition, which will increase your CPC.

The goal of research is to uncover hidden pockets of new keywords for lower than average cost. This can be done in a number of different ways.

Google Analytics

If you do not have Google Analytics set up on your website, stop reading right now and set it up. Understanding your users is incredibly important to running successful AdWords campaigns and is the first step of proficient research.

You can use Google Analytics to find where your most profitable customers are coming from, so you can focus on getting more customers just like them. Use the location and language reports and sort by conversion rate. This will give you a good idea about where you should start you location targeting.

The next report that is beneficial for research is your **Goals** and **E-commerce Reports**. These reports will give you information about which products are best performing - both from a quantity and conversion rate standpoint.

A strategy that can work very well with this report is to find high margin, high converting products or goals that do not get a lot of traffic. You can use AdWords to send more traffic to those pages and, therefore, increase sales.

The **Keyword Report** in Google Analytics is not as beneficial as it used to be, because Google is now providing much less data. Nonetheless, this is another important report to look at when searching for new keywords to add to your campaigns. It provides you with statistics about which keywords are sending the most qualified traffic (time on site, average pages viewed) and which are creating the most sales.

Competitive Research

Understanding what your competitors are doing is important because you can piggyback on their successes and cut some time off of the learning curve of your campaign.

Spyfu and SEMrush are both great tools for doing just that. With these tools, you can input your competitor's URL and they will output different metrics that you can use for your campaigns. Everything from daily spend, to text ads and destination URLs can be seen. A rule of thumb is that if you see your competition's spend increasing over time, it is likely because they are getting positive results. The campaigns with more impressions are also an indicator of good performance.

Google Keyword Planner

Google's Keyword tool is available inside of the AdWords interface under the **Tools** menu item. It has become the default keyword research starting point.

With it, you can input the keywords you think you want to target and it will give you the search volume and competitiveness of that keyword, along with other related keywords that you may want to use. You can sort the columns to find keywords that you may not have thought of previously.

While this is a great starting point, there are other alternatives that can work even better. Keywordtool.io uses Google's **Search Suggest** feature to give you even *more* variations of your keywords. It is an invaluable tool and one that I personally use on every campaign that I create. The second alternative is called KWfinder. The goal of this tool is to help you find long-tail keywords with low competition. These keywords, if used correctly, can be highly profitable.

Talk To Your Customers

The last research method that we will discuss takes us back to the basics of business- talk to your current customers. Reaching out to people that have already purchased your product, whether it be via phone call or e-mail, can provide some of the most insightful data available.

You can ask them *how* they found your product, *what* they call your product and *how* they use it. You can use their reviews to write ads and find new keywords. You will be surprised by some of the unintended uses that users have for your product. Sometimes, it can even open up a whole new sales funnel for you and your company.

For example, if you sell running shoes online and find out that some of your customers are using a specific pair of shoes for CrossFit training, you can begin to advertise those shoes to customers in the CrossFit market.

Online research is great, but sometimes it can fail to make that crucial one-degree-of-separation connection that can open new doors for your business. Talking to your customers can lead to opportunities that research tools cannot.

Review

1. Review your Google Analytics account

2. Leverage what your competitors are already doing

3. Talk to real people

Step 8: Optimizing and Testing

The last section of this book is about optimization and testing - not because they are the least important, but because it should be on the top of your mind when running your next (or first) AdWords campaign. It simply is not good enough to launch a campaign using the strategies that we have discussed and just *hope* your campaign performs well from then on.

I have coached many marketers on the basics of beginning and running campaigns, and I have found that this facet is the hardest to grasp. Very rarely are campaigns going to be performing optimally from the start. For the first month or so, you are looking for a small glimmer that the campaign will eventually be able to perform at scale. This can be as small as one or two conversions that you use to optimize other aspects of the campaign.

From there, you can expand on the positive results and try to find more of the same. Looking for the data points that are unique to those that converted can give you some insight about where to expand and where to pause.

Keywords

Optimization can be an ambiguous word. You obviously want to continue to improve with your campaigns, but this can be done in thousands of different ways. You have to make sure that you are doing it the *best way* possible.

The first way to optimize your campaign is to look at your keywords. The initial plan of attack should be on negative keywords. Keywords that are unrelated to your Ad Groups can cause unwanted impressions and even clicks - which leads to wasted money and a lower Quality Score.

You can find these quickly by going to **Keyword Report** and clicking **Search Terms > All** under the **Details** dropdown. From there, you can easily determine which keywords are not worth spending money on.

Another thing to look for in your campaign's Keyword Report is keywords that have substantially lower click through rates (CTR) than others. An easy way to determine which keywords are underperforming is to look at the average CTR on the top of the report. Consider pausing any keywords that are around twenty percent below the average.

However, make sure to let each keyword get a fair chance before pausing. One hundred impressions is the minimum number to allow before pausing, and more is better.

Another problem that people often complain about with keywords, or testing in general, is that it is hard to understand what is working if you have not received any conversions from your campaigns.

There is another way.

You can use **Engagement Metrics** to see which campaigns, Ad Groups and keywords are driving the most interested users. The metrics to use for this are **Average Session Duration** and **Pages Per Session** - both of which are available inside of Google Analytics.

You can also connect your Google Analytics and AdWords accounts to import the metrics directly into the AdWords interface. This makes analysis quick and easy to do inside your account.

Ad Copy

From a testing and optimization standpoint, Ad Copy can be the easiest component of your campaigns to test. Not only can you try to drive a higher CTR, but you can also test messaging for other uses on your website.

To test, create two ad variations within an Ad Group. Let them run for up to a month, or until they each get an adequate number of impressions. Anywhere from one hundred to two hundred impressions is a good starting point for testing. From there, pause the one that lost the A/B battle and replace it with another challenger.

This should be a continuous process. You will be able to make many improvements in a short amount of time with minimal work.

You can test everything from the headline, to capitalization, to the description lines, to single adjectives. To understand exactly what is working, try to form a hypothesis around one element of the ads and test it. Trying to test multiple elements at once can leave you confused as to which had the most influence on the change.

I have worked with companies that use their branded AdWords campaigns to test brand or product positioning.

To explain how this can be useful, we will use an example with the same shoe company we discussed earlier that has a multipurpose product (running shoes and CrossFit shoes). Multipurpose products can perform well, but this company has decided that they want to hone in on a particular market and they are unsure which market to choose. In addition to running tests on their site's copy with Optimizely (an A/B testing tool), they use AdWords to test two distinct options:

Top ad

Phoots - The world's best marathon shoe.
www.codeschool.com
Free shipping on all orders.

After over 20,000 impressions and a month of monitoring CTR, on-site engagement and conversions, "the world's best marathon shoe" was the clear winner. They decided to use it as their main messaging and created a separate page and campaign to cater to the smaller CrossFit audience.

Landing Pages

A landing page is the page a user gets sent to following a click on your ad and it is the third component that you should be working to improve on a consistent basis. The choice of what pages to use in your campaign are just as vital as the targeting, keywords, and ad copy you set up when launching your campaign.

Customers make a lot of decisions about your company within the first few seconds on your website. Ensure that you are making the best first impression by utilizing testing.

If you are an e-commerce company, try testing category pages versus specific product pages. If you are a service based company, try testing your homepage versus more detailed, long-form pages.

You can even create unique landing pages just for your AdWords campaigns that cater to specific Ad Groups with the goal of being as specific as possible. If you are not well versed in creating webpages, Unbounce is a fantastic drag-and-drop tool for creating high converting landing pages. It also has options for A/B testing page variations, which is really helpful.

It is important that you are comparing apple to apples when testing- meaning, make sure that you are testing landing pages inside the same Ad Groups and, optimally, the same ad. Different ads can attract different customers, which can give different results.

Also, make sure you are getting enough impressions during the test to make a good decision. 200 to 500 impressions is usually a good starting point for low volume campaigns, but for ones with higher traffic, 1,000 impressions is a better barometer.

Retargeting

Retargeting allows you to serve banner ads to people that have previously been to your site. The ads can show up on any site that also uses the Google Display network that the same user visits. These sites include everything from a small cooking blog to the *New York Times*.

Think of it this way: when have you ever bought something online the first time you viewed it? I am guessing the answer is very rarely. With retargeting, you can gently nudge users that showed interest in your company back to your product and try to entice them with another chance to purchase - perhaps with an added discount, if you so choose.

The other great part of retargeting ads is that you can use the pay-per-click cost structure, but you get the benefit of the ad even if the user does not click it. Sometimes, just seeing it again is enough to cause a customer to follow through and add the item to their shopping carts.

There are several places to get banner ads made online if you are not a graphic designer. Rightbanners.com and fiverr.com are some excellent, reasonably priced resources. Elance and oDesk are resources to find more professional freelancing options. If you want to take a crack at designing your own, Canva is a great tool.

No matter what you use, I truly feel that retargeting campaigns are a non-negotiable component to successful AdWords campaigns. They can even turn into your most valuable campaign. Perhaps it even becomes the *only* campaign type you run, but at the very least, it should be running as a supplement to everything else you are doing on AdWords.

Review

     1. Always be testing.

     2. Get enough traffic before making a decision.

     3. Compare apples to apples.

     4. Retarget or die.

The Wrap Up

At the end of the day, AdWords is not as complex as it is often made out to be. This notion may come from the fact that many AdWords users launch a campaign without the right knowledge about how to use it, which leads to poor results. These poor results are perpetuated by the same people telling friends or other businesses that AdWords does not work or it is too difficult to understand. In actuality, it comes down to understanding the options that you have available in your tool belt and understanding how to use those tools to find new customers.

The part that makes AdWords so unique when compared to other marketing and advertising mediums is the specificity and granularity that you can use to target. When you understand how users are searching and what intent those searches hold, you will be able to wield AdWords like a trusty sword.

Scale up or scale back whenever you need, but just know that the power of AdWords is within your reach. Now that you have knowledge of that power, go out there, launch your first campaign and start building your business.

If you're interested in taking the video course that I've made in conjunction with this course, head over to www.googleadwordstutorial.com and use code **'BOOK'** during checkout to get **25% off** the regular price. The course features over two hours of screencasts in a live AdWords account that walk through exactly how to implement each step that I've discussed in this book.

If you have any questions along the way about AdWords or specific questions about your campaigns, please feel free to email me directly (coreyrab@gmail.com) or Tweet me @coreyrab. I am happy to help!

Made in the USA
San Bernardino, CA
11 February 2017